To whom it may concern.

You Have
the Time

Our everyday routines can be so all-encompassing that
we often forget to make room for anything else, including
what we set out to do. Often, the important things get
overlooked, overshadowed by the complexities of the day.
The goal of this book is to clear some space, to provide a
reminder of who you are and what matters to you.

Our lives consist of the small things that fill the everyday.
This book is intended as a reminder of the many options
you always have.

1
DRAW A PICTURE WITH YOUR EYES CLOSED.

2
MAKE A SELF-PORTRAIT.
Use any method or materials you like.

3
DRAW A PICTURE OF A FRIEND.
See how many different ways you can do it.

4

LOOK UP A WORD OR PHRASE YOU'VE NEVER USED BEFORE. TRY USING IT.

5

LOOK UP THE WORDS TO A SONG YOU HALF-REMEMBER.

6

WRITE A REVIEW
of something you like.

7

List the projects you want to work on.

SET A DEADLINE FOR COMPLETING ONE OF THEM.

8

WRITE DOWN EVERYTHING YOU
CAN REMEMBER ABOUT
A PLACE YOU ONCE VISITED.

7/28/11

7/28/11

7/28/11

7/28/11

7/28/11

7/28/11

7/28/11

7/28/11

7/28/11

7/27/11

7/27/11

7/27/11

7/27/11

7/27/11

7/27/11

9

REREAD YOUR DIARY OR JOURNAL.
If you don't keep one,
reread old emails or text messages.

10

DESCRIBE SOMETHING
OR SOMEONE YOU LOVE IN

One page,

one paragraph,

one sentence, or

one word.

11

**Rewrite a story
you were told when you
were young.**

12

FIND A RIDDLE OR A JOKE
TO TELL TO A FRIEND.

knock,
knock

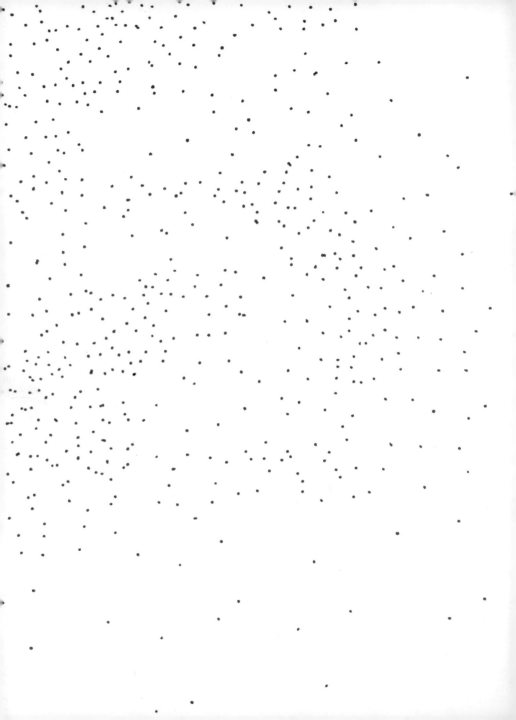

13

OBSERVE THOSE AROUND YOU.
*What do you think they are thinking,
feeling, wanting?*

14

WATCH THE LIGHT
AS IT CHANGES

15

SIT QUIETLY FOR FIVE MINUTES
LISTENING TO THE SOUNDS AROUND YOU.

16
WRITE A LETTER TO
SOMEONE YOU ADMIRE.

*Explain to them
how they've
influenced you.*

17

List all of your interests.

18 PRIORITIZE THEM.

19

Turn a familiar thing upside down.

OR SIDEWAYS.

ROYAL GALA
4173
Product of USA

-XS-
100%
COMBED
COTTON
MADE IN U.S.A.

MAX

MINI STAPLES

No.10-5M

5000 staples

PANTONE®
7464 C

GRAPHITE DRAWING SINCE 1889   4H

Table A1
Party Size: 2
Server: KUNG   Order#: 27
12/11/2012 12:56 PM

-Phad Thai <Togo>
 Chicken
 3***
 Cmt: TO GO

20

Read what's written on things around you:

furniture, clothing, food.

21

22
EXPLORE A BUILDING.
GO TO EVERY FLOOR,
even every room, if you can.

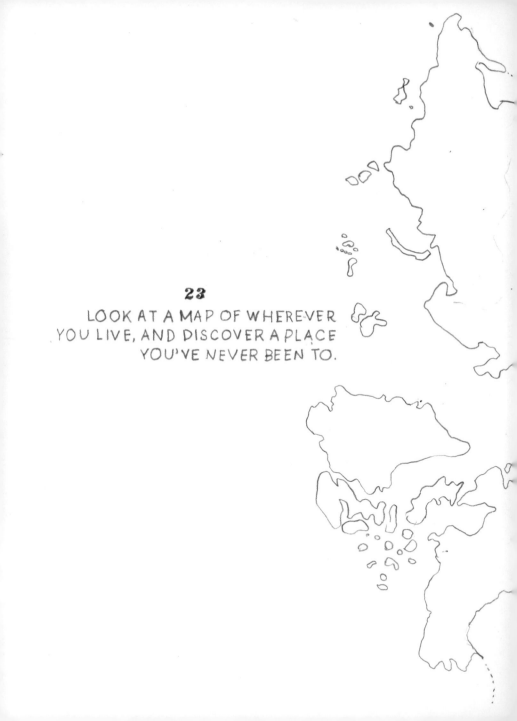

23

LOOK AT A MAP OF WHEREEVER
YOU LIVE, AND DISCOVER A PLACE
YOU'VE NEVER BEEN TO.

24

LOOK UP THE HISTORY
OF YOUR TOWN.

25

RESEARCH WHERE YOUR
SURNAME CAME FROM.

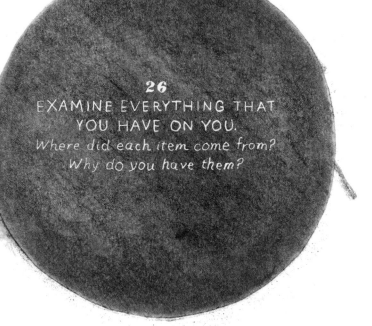

26
EXAMINE EVERYTHING THAT
YOU HAVE ON YOU.
Where did each item come from?
Why do you have them?

27

EXAMINE A NEARBY THING.

Who made it? How? And from what?

29

Relax, rest, stretch.

Breathe
deeply.

Ding, dong!

30
INTRODUCE YOURSELF TO A NEIGHBOR.

31

EXPLORE HOW YOU'RE FEELING
at this moment.

32

INTERVIEW A FRIEND.

Try to discover three things you never knew.

33

HAVE A FRIEND INTERVIEW YOU.

34
MEDITATE.

35
REFUSE THOUGHTS.

36
INVITE THOUGHTS

37
NAME THE MOVIE YOU
MOST WANT TO SEE
BUT HAVEN'T SEEN YET,
then watch it.

38

ASK A FRIEND TO SUGGEST
A MOVIE YOU SHOULD WATCH,
something they think you need
to see. Then watch it.

39
RECOMMEND ONE TO
THEM IN RETURN.

40 Call or write to a friend

YOU HAVEN'T
SPOKEN TO
IN SOME TIME.

41

NAME A BOOK THAT YOU'VE MEANT TO READ FOR YEARS.

What's stopped you so far?

42

READ THAT BOOK.

Read the first and
last pages if nothing else.

43
READ A PAGE OF THE DICTIONARY.

44
INVENT A NEW WORD OR EXPRESSION.

A
B
C
D
E
F
G
H
I
J
K
L
M
N
O
P
Q
R
S
T
U
V
W
X
Y
Z

Bonjour

Oui, oui.

Jambo

HOWDY

Y'all come back now,
ya hear?

hola

45
PRACTICE AN ACCENT.

Spend all day using it.

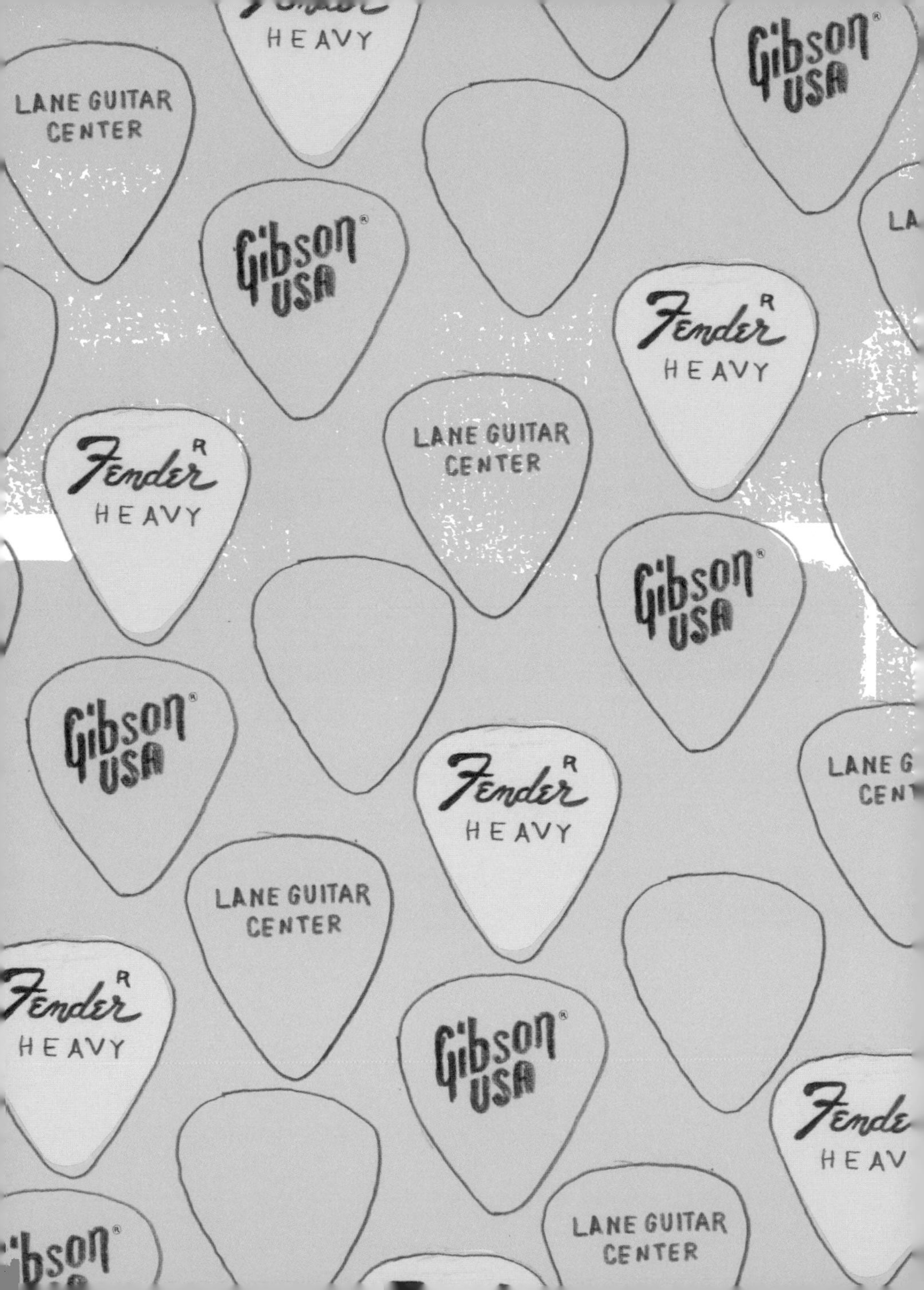

Fender HEAVY
LANE GUITAR CENTER
Gibson USA

46

SIGN UP FOR A NEW CLASS.

47

TRY OUT A NEW DANCE MOVE.

48

TRY PLAYING AN INSTRUMENT
you've never played before.

4

READ A PARAGRAPH FROM ONE BOOK,

9

THEN A PARAGRAPH FROM ANOTHER.
Invent a connection between them.

50
TRY PLAYING A GAME YOU'VE
NEVER PLAYED.

51
PLAY A GAME YOU KNOW WELL,
but change one thing about it

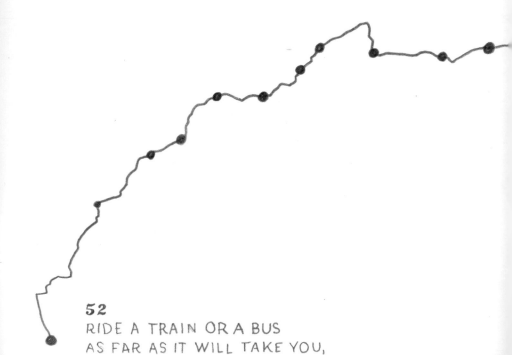

52

RIDE A TRAIN OR A BUS
AS FAR AS IT WILL TAKE YOU,

THEN RIDE IT BACK.

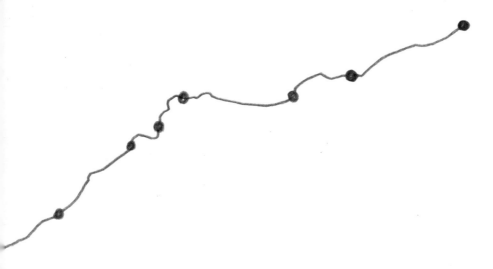

53
INTRODUCE TWO FRIENDS WHO
DON'T KNOW ONE ANOTHER BUT WHO
YOU THINK SHOULD BE FRIENDS.

54

SET UP A SINGLE FRIEND WITH
ANOTHER SINGLE FRIEND.

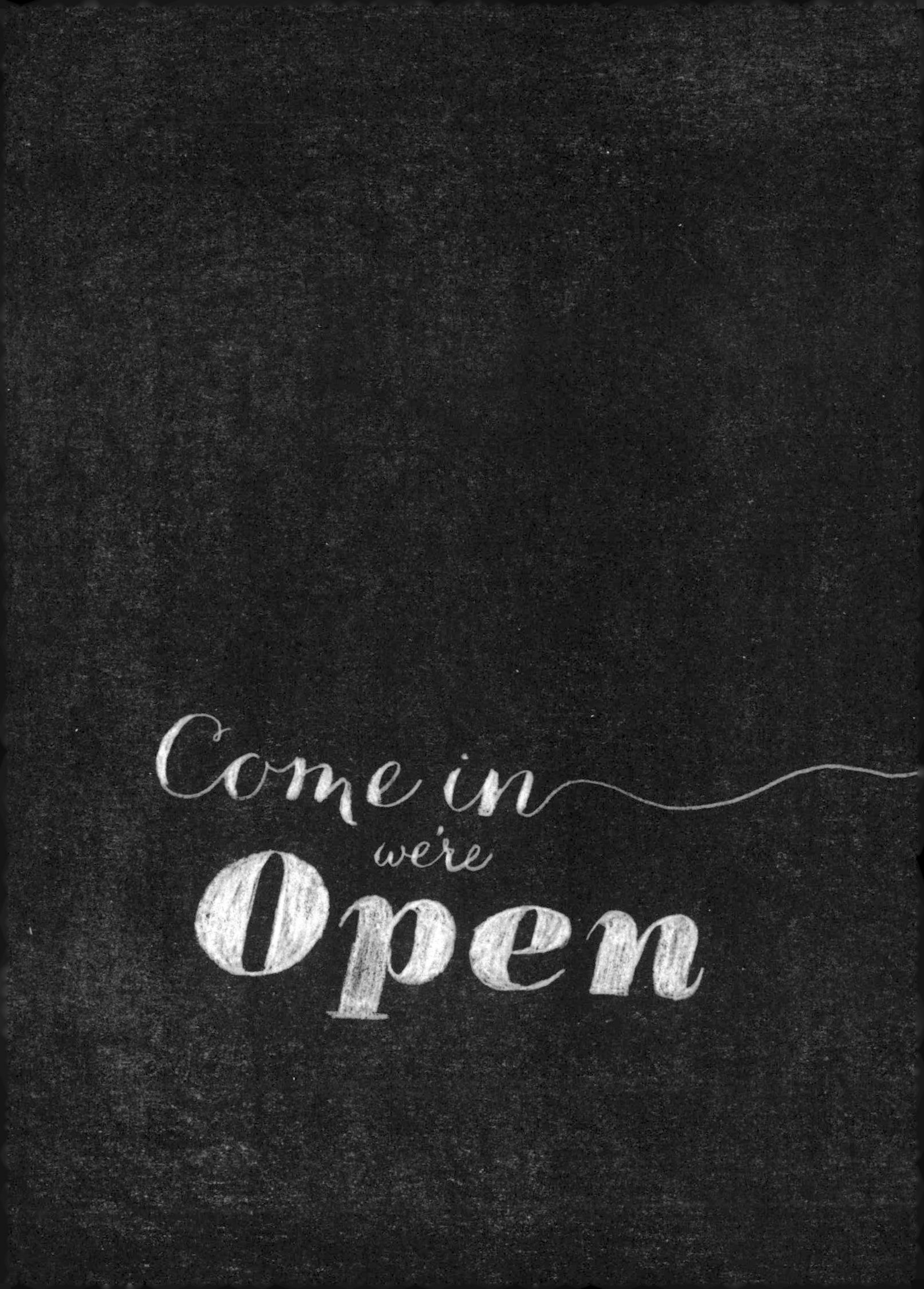
Come in
we're
Open

55

VISIT A LOCAL BUSINESS
YOU'VE WALKED PAST
but haven't gone inside before.

56

START A CONVERSATION WITH
A TOTAL STRANGER.

DATE	ISSUED TO

57

GIVE A BOOK TO A FRIEND,
ONE YOU THINK
WILL CHANGE THEIR LIFE.

58

FIND A COPY OF A FAVORITE BOOK
AT A LIBRARY OR A BOOKSTORE.
Leave a note in it.

59

TURN OFF YOUR CELL PHONE

for an hour, an afternoon, a whole day.

Practice
writing
with your
other hand.

61

SEE HOW LONG YOU CAN
GO WITHOUT SPEAKING.

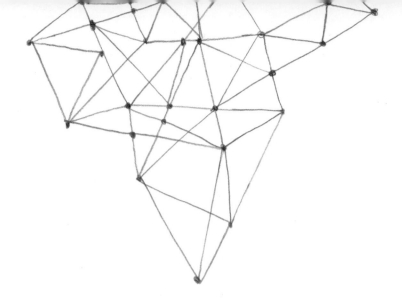

62
READ A RANDOM
WIKIPEDIA ARTICLE.

63
LOOK UP A TOPIC YOU'VE
ALWAYS WANTED
TO BETTER UNDERSTAND.

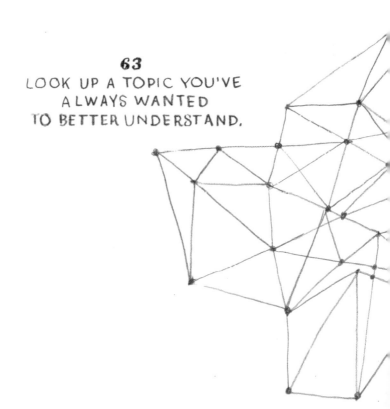

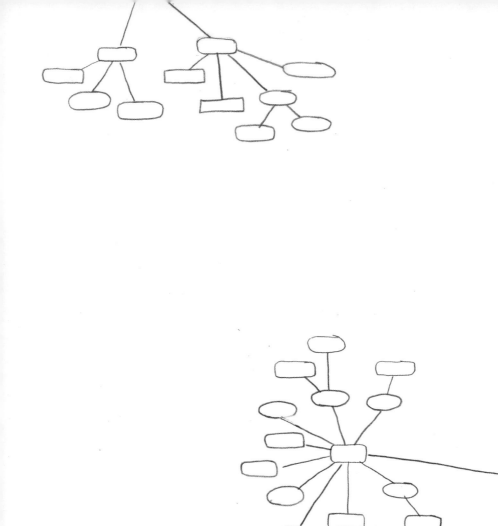

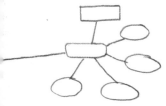

64

LEARN HOW TO FIX A SMALL
PROBLEM THAT SOMEONE'S
BEEN HAVING.

3—
#860

65

Listen to an album that was once important to you

THAT YOU HAVEN'T HEARD IN YEARS.

66

Describe yourself the way a loved one would describe you.

67

KEEP A DIARY,
even if only for a day.

68

WRITE DOWN THE NAME
OF EVERY CITY YOU HAVE
EVER BEEN TO.

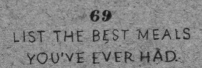

69
LIST THE BEST MEALS
YOU'VE EVER HAD.

70
FAST.

7.1

EAT SOMETHING YOU'VE
NEVER EATEN BEFORE,
especially if it's a vegetable
or a fruit.

72

TRY EATING A FOOD YOU'VE
MADE UP YOUR MIND YOU
DON'T LIKE.

73

Cook a meal

FOR A FRIEND.

74
GIVE SOMETHING PRECIOUS
TO A FRIEND.

75

Take a long bath, the longest bath that you've ever taken.

76

GET A MAP AND MARK THE PLACES YOU'VE BEEN.

77
GO SOMEWHERE FAMILIAR BY MEANS
OF AN UNFAMILIAR ROUTE.

Pick a simple

78

task and do it as simply as you can.

79

OBSERVE THE FACE YOU TEND TO MAKE.

Try making a different face.

80

Do yoga.

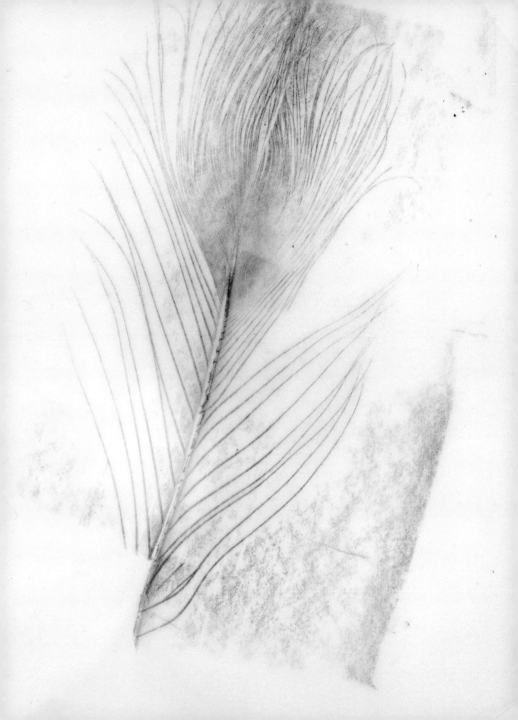

81

Do something that you think you cannot do.

82

STAND ON A STREET
WATCHING CARS THAT PASS.

Where is everyone going?

83

PUT ON AN ARTICLE OF CLOTHING YOU
NEVER WEAR ANYMORE.

84

GET RID OF SOMETHING YOU
NO LONGER NEED.
Give it to someone who needs it.

85
PICK A COLOR.
NOTE WHEREVER IT APPEARS.

86
STUDY A TREE
OR PLANT INTENTLY.

87
PLANT A SEED.

88
WRITE DOWN YOUR
EARLIEST MEMORIES.

89
ASK SOMEONE OLDER THAN YOU
TO DESCRIBE WHAT THE WORLD WAS
LIKE BEFORE YOU WERE BORN.

90

ASK A CHILD TO EXPLAIN
SOMETHING TO YOU. REALLY
LISTEN TO WHAT THEY SAY.

91
DO SOMETHING
YOU HATE.

FIND A WAY
OF DOING IT
SO THAT YOU
LIKE IT,

even love it.

Resolve to

change
something
about
yourself.

93

THINK ABOUT WHERE
YOU WOULD LIKE TO BE IN  YEARS.

THINK ABOUT WHERE
YOU'D LIKE TO BE IN

50

95

*Finish something
you've given
up all hope of ever
completing.*

96
ENJOY THE FEEL OF THE WEATHER,
whatever it currently is.

97

*Realize that you
have time.*

STRIVE TO BE **98** *happy.*

List

99

more things to do when
you have the time.

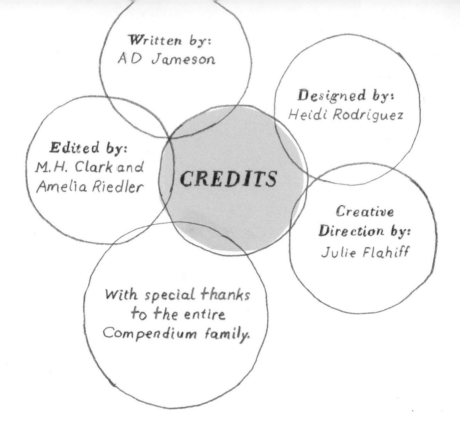

CREDITS

Written by:
AD Jameson

Designed by:
Heidi Rodriguez

Edited by:
M.H. Clark and
Amelia Riedler

Creative
Direction by:
Julie Flahiff

With special thanks
to the entire
Compendium family.

ISBN: 978-1-935414-86-5

1st printing. Printed in China with soy and metallic inks.

COMPENDIUM®
INCORPORATED

live inspired.®

ISBN 978-193541486-5

PRINTED IN CHINA WITH SOY AND METALLIC INKS. LIVE-INSPIRED.COM